This book belongs to:

....

A Bowyer Book
Published in the United Kingdom
by Bowyer Publishing in 2018
Copyright © Paquita Lamacraft
All rights reserved
The moral right of the author has been asserted.

This book is presented for information and entertainment
purposes only. The information presented herein represents the
view of the author at date of publication. The author reserves the
right to alter and update opinions based on new information and
new conditions. While every attempt has been made to verify
the information in this book, neither the author nor affiliates/
partners assume any responsibility for errors, inaccuracies,
or omissions. At no time can any of the information herein be
construed as professional, investment, tax, accounting, or legal
advice, nor does it constitute a recommendation or warrant of
suitability for any particular business, industry, transaction, or
business strategy.

ISBN: 9781999627317
Cover Image Extended Content License Agreement
iStock – Getty Images

Author's Web Address: www.paquitalamacraft.com
Bowyer Publishing- A Division of Archer Business Group
PO Box 666, Eastleigh, Hampshire, England SO50 0PA

The quotations in this book are drawn from those used in my book 'Shrapnel Free Explosive Growth: How to be your own Business Advisor to manage growth.'

This little book distils a great deal of wisdom in the quotes themselves but it also gives a broader insight into the character and achievements of those who made them. Some of them are mine directly. I hope you find them all enjoyable, thought provoking, and worth their print space!

Please adopt those that have deeper meaning for you so you can extend the use of positive quotations in a world where positives seem sometimes a threatened species.

Paquita

*"Knock Knock.
Who's there?*

Opportunity.

*Don't be silly – opportunity
doesn't knock twice!"*

Anon

*"Start where you are.
Use what you have.
Do what you can."*

Arthur Ashe

Ashe was the first black tennis player on the US Davis Cup Team and the only black man to ever win the singles of Wimbledon, The Australian Open, and the US Open. A shy and retiring man, he was nevertheless outspoken on issues of race and prejudice. Sadly, he contracted HIV from contaminated blood during bypass surgery. Before his death at age 49, he used his fame to help others suffering with HIV AIDS.

From a disadvantaged background and with a mother who died when he was just six, Ashe started playing tennis on a segregated tennis playground close to his Virginia home. By the time he was 14 he came to the attention of a Lynchburg physician who became his patron, having assisted other black tennis prodigies for over 20 years.

Ashe used his tennis scholarship to U.C.L.A. not just to be a member of the Davis Cup team, but to graduate with a BS in Business Administration. He was still in his three year military service when he was the first black tennis player to win a Grand Slam event when he won the US Open at Forest Hills.

Memorably, in 1975 he defeated Jimmy Connors at the Wimbledon final. It was reported that he drove Connors to be even more manic than usual by calmly meditating between changeovers.

> *"We are stuck
> with technology
> when what we really want
> is just stuff that works."*

Douglas Adams

Douglas Adams is well known for his wry humour in books like "The Hitchhiker's Guide to the Galaxy" which was originally a BBC Radio 4 series, "The Long Dark Tea-Time of the Soul" and "So Long and Thanks For All the Fish."

Written in conjunction with John Lloyd, "The Meaning of Liff" takes odd sounding English place names and gives them wonderful new meanings: GWEEK (n.) A coat hanger recycled as a car aerial; MOTSPUR (n.) The 4th wheel of a supermarket trolley which looks identical to the other three but renders the trolley completely uncontrollable; HAPPLE (vb.) To annoy people by finishing their sentences for them and then telling them what they really meant to say; SOLENT (adj.) Description of the state of serene self-knowledge reached through drink.

Adams wrote for the TV series "Doctor Who" and gained a writing credit for the Monty Python sketch "Patient Abuse", also writing the Marilyn Monroe sketch on the soundtrack of "Monty Python and the Holy Grail."

A fervent atheist, he lived by this belief:

"To give real service
you must add something
which cannot be bought
or measured with money,
and that is sincerity and integrity."

*"Chaos is merely order
waiting
to be deciphered."*

José Saramago - The Double

José de Sousa Saramago was a Portuguese novelist and social activist and winner of the 1998 Nobel Prize for Literature. His allegorical writing had its own peculiarities of style that led him to receive many awards and the respect of an international audience.

Saramango was a committed communist and as the son of impoverished farmers it is unsurprising that his writings reflect social inequities. He was also an atheist but one whose attitude to religion was precise:

"I respect those who believe, but I have no respect for the institution."

"Chase two rabbits and both will escape."

Anon

"Learn from rock climbers:
If something is critical,
three points of contact
are a good idea."

Paquita Lamacraft from
'Shrapnel Free Explosive Growth'

"Simplicity is about subtracting the obvious and adding the meaningful."

John Maeda

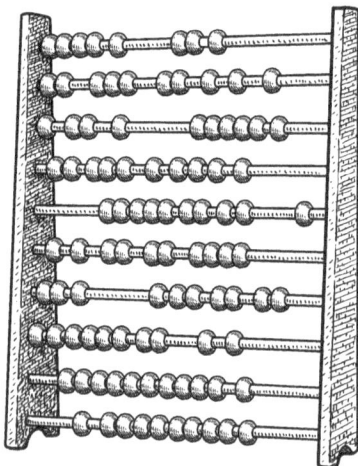

In 1999 John Maeda was named by Esquire Magazine as one of the 21 most important people in the 21st century.

As a Professor at MIT Labs over 12 years, he developed a collaborative community of engineers who could design, and designers who could code, resulting in unusually creative technology crossover. The organisations he later led were globally recognised for their insightful forward thinking.

Maeda has long advocated a change of focus from just STEM subjects (Science, Technology, Engineering, and Maths) to also including Art.

His best-selling book 'Laws of Simplicity,' published in 2006 is still a key handbook on effective design: for organisational systems, physical things, technology, or life as lived. Some of its thoughts include:

- Where there is less, we appreciate everything much more.
- To simplify, you must achieve a sort of state of enlightened shallowness that softens the intensity of focus.
- A certain kind of more is better than less: more care, more love, more meaningful actions.

*"All things being equal,
people will
do business with a friend;
all things being unequal,
people will still
do business with a friend."*

Mark McCormack

Mark McCormack was an American lawyer who founded the International Management group (IMG) to connect celebrities and sports figures with endorsements and sponsorship. He was the first to see the potential of using endorsements as an income stream and his early clients were the first to do so: Arnold Palmer, Gary Player, and Jack Nicklaus. Later the famous names included tennis stars Rod Laver, Billie Jean King, Chris Evert, Björn Borg, Pete Sampras and Monica Seles.

In 1990, Sporting News named him as the 'Most Powerful Man in Sports'. In 1992 The Times of London named him one of "A Thousand People Who Most Influenced the 20th Century."

He wrote *'What they Don't Teach you at Harvard Business School'* and its sequel *'What they STILL Don't...',* and *'Never Wrestle with a Pig and Ninety Other Ideas to Build Your Business and Career'.*

*"If you don't like
what you see in the mirror
when you are honest
in describing your company
as it operates today,
don't look for another
mirror.*

Fix the reflection."

Paquita Lamacraft from
'Shrapnel Free Explosive Growth'

*"T stands for Technology -
not trauma!"*

Paquita Lamacraft from
'Shrapnel Free Explosive Growth'

*"A person's a person,
no matter how small."*

Dr. Seuss

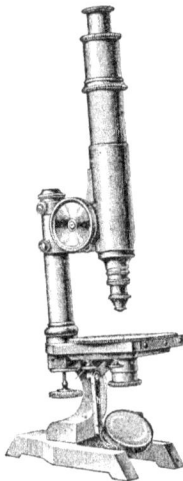

Theodor Seuss Geisel, American author, political cartoonist, poet, animator, book publisher and artist. He is best known for his books (more than 60) written under the pen name Doctor Seuss.

He is a model for all about working from your passion: leaving university without a degree he managed to support his family, even throughout the Great Depression, through illustrating and writing.

He was an early success at combining theatre and comedy as a way to make advertising memorable. Later, during World War II he became a political cartoonist for the war effort.

At the end of the war, the educational director of Houghton Mifflin publishing house was distressed to read of the increasing illiteracy of the nation's children. This was attributed to boredom in the books they were given, so he compiled a list of 380 words that he thought to be important for first graders to understand. Geisel was given the challenge to cut this to 250 words and write en engaging children's story using them – and so emerged "The Cat in the Hat." This is how Geisel turned to writing for children.

Geisel had no children of his own and used to say: "You have 'em; I'll entertain 'em." In 1956 he was awarded an honorary Doctorate from Dartmouth, the University he had left without a degree.

*"I hire people
brighter than me
and I get out of their way."*

Lee Iacocca

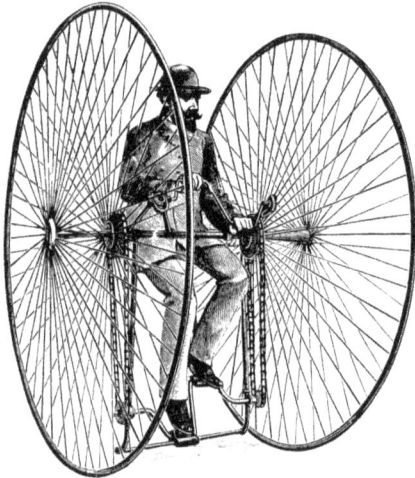

Lee Iacocca worked his way up in Ford as an engineering graduate, moving into sales before becoming a VP and Divisional Manager. His style clashed with that of Henry Ford II, who fired him.

Iacocca became a legendary business leader when he led an almost bankrupt Chrysler Corporation to record profits in the 1980s, leaving it in 1992.

He wrote that our leaders should have: curiosity, creativity, communication, character, courage, conviction, charisma, competence and common sense – and laments the departure of these qualities in leadership.

Iacocca's beloved wife died of diabetes leading him to fund research into the disease through establishment of a Family Foundation. Royalties from his books contribute to it.

"Digital Natives who are not trained to do otherwise, fit the task to the tool.

You need to have people fit the right tool to the task."

Paquita Lamacraft from
'Shrapnel Free Explosive Growth'

> *"When dealing with the press choose your own platform. If the national press wants to move you to another, just keep bouncing back to the one you choose.*
>
> *If you haven't defined it beforehand you may end up where you don't want to be."*

Paquita Lamacraft from
'Shrapnel Free Explosive Growth'

*"It is the obvious
that is so difficult to see
most of the time.*

*People say
'It's as plain
as the nose on your face.'*

*But how much
of the nose on your face
can you see
unless someone
holds a mirror up to you?"*

Isaac Asimov in 'I, Robot'

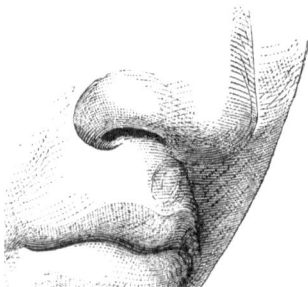

Isaac Asimov was born into a milling family on what is now the Belarus Russian border. He emigrated with his family at age three and became a naturalised American citizen at age eight. After teaching himself to read at age five, his passion for reading was furnished with daily new material as his family had a small candy store selling magazines and newspapers.

He later earned a Masters degree in Chemistry, served three years at the Philadelphia Navy Yard's Naval Experimental Station and then went on to a PhD in Biochemistry. After being drafted into the US Army in 1945 he was saved by a bureaucratic error from being on the task force to Bikini Atoll for the now infamous nuclear tests. By the time he became a tenured faculty member at Boston University Medical School he was earning more from his writing.

Apart from his science fiction, Asimov wrote on a wide range of non-fiction subjects. He has bequeathed us with new words that seem here to stay: 'robotics' and 'positronic'. Like Arthur Ashe he contracted HIV from blood transfusions during a heart bypass operation.

Carl Sagan and Marvin Minsky, the computer scientist involved with Artificial Intelligence, were the two people Asimov had met whom he felt had intellect beyond his own.

*"Rowing harder doesn't help
if the boat is headed
in the wrong direction."*

Kenichi Ohmae

Kenichi Ohmae was trained as a nuclear scientist but is best known for his thinking about strategy. A polymath in a country known for specialist focus, Ohmae is an accomplished flautist, has a love of motorcycles, and includes martial arts and scuba diving amongst his hobbies.

His 1982 book "The Mind of the Strategist," gives insight on those who built great global Japanese companies, showing that they used only practical experience, vision and intuition rather than academic learning His further writing of over 100 books includes "Triad Power: The Coming Shape of Global Competition" in 1985, "The Borderless World: Power and strategy in the interlinked economy" in 1990, and in 1995 "The End of the Nation State". This previous prescient thinking may give us pause to ponder his thoughts on economic protectionism:

"If patriotism is, as Dr. Johnson used to remark, the last refuge of the scoundrel, wrapping outdated industry in the mantle of national interest is the last refuge of the economically dispossessed.

In economic terms, pleading national interest is the declining cottage industry of those who have been bypassed by the global economy."

*"Identities
are the beginning
of everything.*

*They are how something is
recognized and understood.*

*What could be
better than that?"*

Paula Scher

Paula Scher designed the brand identity for the Museum of Modern Art (MoMA) and has created logos for Microsoft and the New York City Ballet. Her work seems always to be at the forefront of design.

Her trend spotting is informed by this thought process:

"If you look through design history and you see something that looks really radical, that's what you're going to be doing now. If you think that's nice, that's what you've already been doing. If you think it's tired, that's what you were doing five years ago. But if you think it's ugly, that's what you're going to be doing in five years."

Paula has donated her services to those whose ethos she values but who cannot afford her, is genuine in saying what she thinks at the risk of political correctness, and is said to have a 'zealous and thoughtful personality'.

*"When your very existence
is threatened,
you have to change.*

*This is one of the hardest
lessons to learn in business,
because it's so
counter-intuitive.
Plus...
it's just plain hard to do."*

Sir Richard Branson

Richard Branson usually needs no introduction: entrepreneur, successful leader of a business empire, adventurer, and philanthropist. What marks him out is his ability to be uniquely himself in a non-abrasive way.

He epitomises 'authenticity':His tribute to his furry friend Sumo, the Irish Water Spaniel-Labrador-cross who just parted from this life to chase seagulls in the sky, takes equal space on the Virgin website as an article on harnessing hyperconnectivity.

"A complex system that works is invariably found to have evolved from a simple system that worked.

A complex system designed from scratch never works and cannot be patched up to make it work.

You have to start over, beginning with a working simple system."

John Gall - Gall's Law

John Gall was a well respected paediatrician and writer of scientific papers and journals, with a focus on the behavioural and developmental problems of children. This led him to question why some systems fail and some work. His collection of examples of systems failures formed a series entitled "Laws of Systems" which was published in 1975 as "Systemantics: How systems work and especially how they fail". This was followed by two more in the series and these have influenced many scientists, systems designers and computer engineers.

It is important to note that the quotation above is preceded by:

"A simple system may or may not work."

In other words do the simplest things first and add features later – or "Fail Small. Learn Big."

In 2001 Gall retired as a doctor after 40 years in practice.

"...welcome to my house.

Come freely.
Go safely;
and leave something
of the happiness you bring."

Bram Stoker

Bram Stoker author of Dracula was an Irish writer whose day job was as manager of the Lyceum, one of the most important of London's theatres at the time. He was also personal secretary to the owner, Henry Irving, and in his company travelled the world, visiting the White House and knowing both Presidents McKinley and Roosevelt.

Stoker was bedridden with childhood illness until he was seven. Making a recovery he later graduated from Trinity College with honours in mathematics.

Employed as a civil servant at Dublin Castle for 10 years, Stoker was at the same time writing as a journalist, and after reviewing Sir Henry Irving's performance in Hamlet, they became friends. This led to over 30 years of management at the Lyceum Theatre.

He wrote 12 novels but didn't live to see the success of his most famous, Dracula. He died in shaky financial circumstances after battling ill health.

*"If you cry 'forward',
you must without fail
make plain
in what direction to go."*

Anton Chekhov

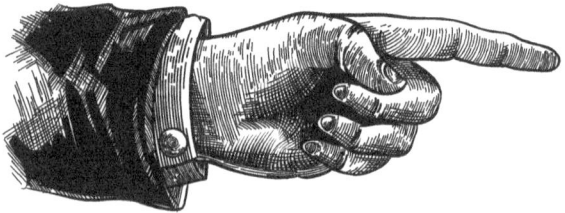

Before Tuberculosis took his life at the age of 44, Anton Chekhov proved to have deep insight into the often masked inner turmoil that haunts many people.

After a harshly disciplined childhood and having to pay for his own education following his father's bankruptcy that left the family in poverty, Chekhov originally wrote for financial gain. However, when he became a physician he said: "Medicine is my lawful wife and literature is my mistress."

His short stories and plays showed a development of a unique style that teetered between comedy and tragedy and showed how the ordinary can have layers of meaning. The realism of his character portrayal in his plays formed the basis of what we now recognise as theatre. Until then characters didn't speak and act as they would in real life.

His dramatic principle was that every element of the narrative must pay its way – and everything superfluous be removed.

"Elegant means shedding everything superfluous and ending up with streamlined and functional.

Elegant should prove pleasing to those who encounter it in whatever capacity they do."

Paquita Lamacraft from
'Shrapnel Free Explosive Growth'

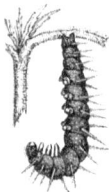

*"Most of us know
what we want
by seeing a lot of
what we don't want."*

Paquita Lamacraft from
'Shrapnel Free Explosive Growth'

*"We cannot do everything
at once,
but we can do something
at once."*

Calvin Coolidge

As Vice President of the United States, Calvin Coolidge became President with the unexpected death of President Warren Harding. He served one term and declined to run for a second.

His policies have been viewed in extremes. During the response to the great flood of the Mississippi in 1927 Coolidge appointed Hoover to be in charge – and has since been saddled with the legacy of Hoover's actions in the ensuing flooding of black communities to save white ones and a series of outrages against the black population.

Coolidge himself refused to appoint any member of the Klu Klux Klan to any senior appointment, appointed black officials, was an active advocate of anti-lynching wars, and granted full citizenship rights to Native Americans.

*"The most serious mistakes
are not being made
as a result of wrong answers.*

*The truly dangerous thing
is asking
the wrong questions."*

Peter Drucker - Men, Ideas & Politics

Widely known and respected for his thinking about management and how it should form the world, Peter Drucker wrote over 39 books and published articles and thought pieces regularly.

The first to recognise management as a function in its own right, Drucker's thinking adapted with the changing times – sometimes refuting his own earlier thoughts.

As a consultant he claimed his greatest strength was in ignorance and asking a few questions.

He worked extensively with non-profit organisations and once named the best manager in the USA at the time as the leader of the Girl Scouts of America. He pointed out that managers in this sector have to be great leaders as their staff are all volunteers.

*"You don't learn
how birds fly
by studying feathers.*

*You need to study
aerodynamics."*

David Marr

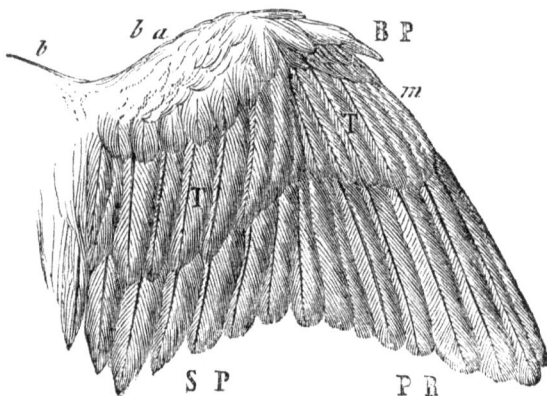

British neuroscientist David Marr influenced the early development of computational neuroscience by combining results from psychology, artificial intelligence, and neurophysiology to develop new models of visual processing.

Marr stressed the importance of avoiding theoretical debates in favour of focusing on exploring and understanding specific problems. His key legacy may be that 'the understanding of any information processing system is incomplete without insight into the problems it faces, and without a notion of the form that possible solutions to these problems can take'.

Sadly, he died of leukaemia at the age of 35.

*"Leaders get out in front
and stay there
by raising the standards
by which
they judge themselves –
and by which they are
willing to be judged."*

Frederick W. Smith,
founder of FedEx

"Fred" Smith conceived the idea of a centralised clearing house for packages while at University and refined it as a Marine Ground Controller flying thousands of hours with navy pilots in the Vietnam War. The idea first appeared in a University paper for which he reputedly didn't even get a C grade – because the professor told him that to get a ' C ' the idea would have to be plausible.

The first ten years of his life was spent crippled from a bone disease, but recovering from that Smith became a football player and also learned to fly at the age of fifteen. His two tours during the Vietnam War were as an airborne ground controller and as such he observed many missions, narrowly missing death when caught in a Vietcong ambush. Smith credits the Marine Corp in teaching him how to treat others and how to be a leader.

Famously, faced with crippling debt Smith gambled at blackjack in Las Vegas and immediately cabled his winnings back to the company.

*"If 'Plan A' fails
there are 25 other letters
in the alphabet."*

Anon

www.ingramcontent.com/pod-product-compliance
Lightning Source LLC
Chambersburg PA
CBHW031910200326
41597CB00012B/577